Look What Came From Austria

Austria

by
Kevin Davis

Franklin Watts
A Division of Scholastic Inc.
New York Toronto London Auckland Sydney
Mexico City New Delhi Hong Kong
Danbury, Connecticut

Series Concept: Shari Joffe
Design: Steve Marton

Library of Congress Cataloging-in-Publication Data

Davis, Kevin.
  Look What Came From Austria / by Kevin Davis.
    p. cm. - (Look what came from series)
  Includes bibliographical references and index.
  Summary: Describes many things that originally came
from Austria, including inventions, music, sports and
games, medical advances, foods, animals, and holidays.
    ISBN 0-531-11958-0 (lib. bdg.)   0-531-16627-9 (pbk.)
    1. Civilization, Modern-Austrian influences-Juvenile
literature.2. Austria-Civilization-Juvenile literature.
[1.Civilization, Modern-Austrian influences.
Austria-Civilization.]
  I. Title. II. Series.

DB30.D39 2002
909.82-dc21   2001046779

Photographs © 2002: American Kennel Club, Inc./Tara Darling: 23 left;
Archive Photos/Getty Images: 6 left, 9 top center, 13 top right (Hulton Getty
Picture Library), 6 background, 17 bottom right; Art Resource, NY/Réunion des
Musées Nationaux/Michele Bellot: 10 left; Austrian National Tourist Office:
21 right (Barti), 12 (Ebersberg), 11 left (Trumler), 24 right (H. Wiesenhofer);
Bruce Coleman Inc./Norman O. Tomalin: 14 right; Corbis Images: 3, 6 right,
7 right, 8 left, 9 bottom center (Archivo Iconografico, S.A.), 7 left, 9 right,
9 left, 13 left, 15 left, 16 (Bettmann), 22 (Jerry Cooke), 24 left, 25 right,
25 left (Marc Garanger), 8 right, 17 left (Hulton-Deutsch Collection),
32 left (Douglas Kirkland), 10 right (K.M. Westermann), 13 bottom right,
14 left; DK Images/Tracy Morgan: 1, 23 right; Envision: 4 (Curzon Studio),
18 right (George Mattei), cover top right, 20 (Steven Needham), 19 (Sharon
Smith); Nance S. Trueworthy: 27 top right, 27 bottom right, 27 left;
National Geographic Image Collection: 15 right (Ned M. Seidler), 21 left
(James L. Stanfield), 18 left (Volkmar K. Wentzel); Photri Inc.: borders, back
cover, cover bottom left; Stone/Getty Images/Doug Armand: cover background;
Superstock, Inc.: 17 top right.

Map by Lisa Jordan

Contents

Greetings from Austria! 4

Music 6

Sports 12

Science 14

Food 18

Animals 22

Holidays 24

A Recipe from Austria 26

How Do You Say . . . ? 28

To Find Out More 29

Glossary 30

Index 31

Greetings from Austria!

Austria is a beautiful country in central Europe. It is a land of snowcapped mountains, tall forests, and open plains. It is a diverse and fascinating place with old castles, big cities, and small villages. Some amazing things have come from Austria, from classical music to delicious foods.

Many different people have lived in Austria during its history. The country has had many wars and invasions. Celts, Romans, Germans, Hungarians, and others have called Austria home.

Austria is next to Germany. The two countries have close ties and were once under the same rule. In fact, their history is tied together so closely that the people of Austria speak German.

So let's take a trip to Austria and see what came from there!

The flag of Austria

Music

Wolfgang Amadeus Mozart at age 9

Although classical music was not invented in Austria, Austria is famous for being a place where a lot of classical music was created. Many classical composers lived and worked in the Austrian city of Vienna in the 1700s and 1800s. People from all over Europe came to Vienna to hear this beautiful music.

One of the best-known composers from Austria was **Wolfgang Amadeus Mozart.** He began to play the piano when he was only 4 years old! He also learned to play the organ and violin. When he was 8, he composed his first

Illustration of the character Papageno from Mozart's opera *The Magic Flute*

Ludwig van Beethoven

Ludwig van Beethoven playing piano for Mozart in Austria

symphony, and when he was 12, he wrote an opera! One of his most famous operas was *The Magic Flute*.

Another well-known composer from Austria was Ludwig van Beethoven. He was born in Germany, but moved to Vienna when he was 22.

You may be familiar with his Fifth Symphony, one of his most famous works. He wrote it about 200 years ago.

People waltzing in Europe in the 1800s

more music

The **waltz** is a dance that came from Austria. People in the countryside were the first to dance the waltz. It later became popular in other places after a composer named **Johann Strauss Sr.** composed special music for the waltz. His son, **Johann Strauss Jr.**, also composed waltzes, including the famous *The Blue Danube*.

Johann Strauss Sr.

Other famous composers who came from Austria include **Franz Joseph Haydn, Johannes Brahms, Gustav Mahler,** and **Franz Schubert.** They all have made great contributions to classical music.

8

Johann Strauss Jr. (left) and Johannes
Brahms (right)

Franz Joseph Haydn

Gustav Mahler

Franz Schubert

9

Accordion

An Austrian girl playing an accordion

even more music

The **accordion** was invented about 200 years ago in Austria. It has a bellows that blows air into metal reeds to make sound. Modern accordions have keyboards like a piano. An inventor named Damian was said to have made the first accordion.

Austria is the home of one of the world's most famous church singing groups. The **Vienna Boy's Choir** was formed about 500 years ago. The choir began when twelve boys sang for Austria's Emperor Maximilian I. Today, the choir includes boys who range in

The Vienna Boy's Choir

Cover of sheet music for "Silent Night"

age from 8 to 13 years old. They perform their beautiful songs all over the world. They also sing every Sunday at a church in Vienna.

One of the world's best-known Christmas songs also came from Austria. "Silent Night," sung around the world, was written nearly 200 years ago. It was created almost by accident.

Some mice had chewed through the bellows of an organ on Christmas Eve. The organ could not be played, so a schoolmaster named Franz Gruber composed a Christmas song for the guitar. A priest named Joseph Mohr wrote the words. Can you figure out why they called the song "Silent Night"?

11

Alpine skiers today

Sports

Most of Austria is covered with beautiful mountains called the Alps. It was on these mountains that the sport of snow skiing first became popular about 100 years ago.

People have used skis for thousands of years to help them get across snow more easily. But the first skiers did not consider skiing a sport. It was just another form of transportation. Some people in Austria thought they could improve the way people used skis and make skiing more fun.

Matthias Zdarsky of Austria is considered the father of modern downhill skiing. In the 1800s, he came up with the idea of people using shorter skis and holding two poles for better control and balance. Zdarsky also designed some of the earliest metal ski bindings. Until that time, people had fastened

Early skis with leather ski bindings (above) and modern-day skis with metal-and-plastic bindings (bottom right)

Hannes Schneider

their boots to their skis with leather straps. Metal bindings held people's boots onto their skis more firmly.

Zdarsky also came up with new ways of turning and stopping on skis. Many people believe he was the world's first ski instructor. He helped make skiing popular in Austria and around the world.

About 20 years later, an Austrian named Hannes Schneider improved the skiing methods taught by Zdarsky. At his Arlberg ski school in Austria, Schneider taught thousands of people to ski for pleasure. His first rule of skiing was to be safe rather than go fast. By making skiing less dangerous, more people could enjoy it! Schneider helped make skiing popular in the United States.

13

Science

Paracelsus (far left) paved the way for modern-day chemical medicines, such as aspirin (left)

People who are sick or have health problems sometimes need to take medicine. In Salzburg in the 1500s, a Swiss-born scientist named Paracelsus was the first person to use **chemicals in medicine.** Before that, most medicines were made from plants. Today, people rely on chemical medicines for everything from treating infections to helping their hearts.

When you visit the doctor, he or she may tap your chest. An Austrian doctor named Leopold Auenbrugger invented this **chest-tapping** technique about 240 years ago. He discovered that by listening to the sounds of the chest while tapping on it, he could tell whether the person was healthy. A hollow sound meant the person was in good health. A dull sound meant that the person's chest might be filled with fluid.

Did you know that the color of your hair or eyes is something you inherit from your parents? In the 1800s, an Austrian monk named Gregor Mendel discovered an important science called **genetics.** This science explains how certain characteristics of living things are passed from parent to offspring. Mendel grew peas in his garden and discovered that their color and size were determined by parent peas.

Gregor Mendel

15

more science

Karl Landsteiner

Do you know what your blood type is? For thousands of years, people did not know that there were different blood types. In the early 1900s, an Austrian scientist named Karl Landsteiner tested blood samples. He found that they had different characteristics. He divided the samples into groups A, B, O, and AB.

A person who is injured and loses a large amount of blood might need a blood transfusion. But a blood transfusion can be dangerous if a person with one blood type receives blood from a person of another blood type. Landsteiner's **blood typing** paved the way for blood transfusions to be carried out safely. This helped save thousands of lives during World War II.

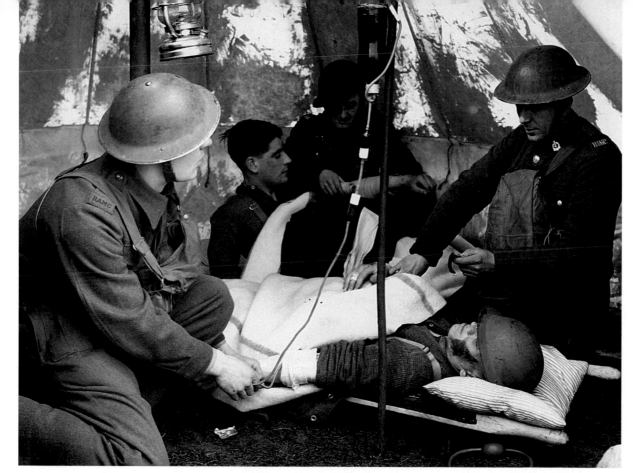

British soldier receiving a blood transfusion during World War II

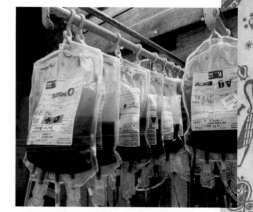

Blood to be used for transfusions

When people get depressed or have lots of worries, they sometimes see a psychiatrist. About 100 years ago, a doctor in Austria developed **psychoanalysis,** a method to help such people. Sigmund Freud believed that people's emotional problems often come from ideas and memories that they're not aware of—a part of the mind Freud called the unconscious. He also believed that people's dreams could help explain their problems.

Sigmund Freud

17

Food

Salt is used all over the world and comes from many sources. But the first big **salt mines** were operated in Austria thousands of years ago. The mines are near the city of Salzburg. In fact, *Salzburg* means "city of salt." The salt that came from the mines near Salzburg was delivered to many other countries.

A salt mine near Salzburg in the 1700s

Salt

Viennese coffee being served at a café in Vienna

Viennese coffee is served around the world. This Austrian treat was first made more than 300 years ago by a Turkish man who moved to Vienna and opened a coffee house. He made his coffee by filtering out the grounds, sweetening it, and adding a bit of milk.

more food

Croissant

When people think of croissants, they usually think of France. But croissants were actually first made in Vienna about 140 years ago. Bakers created the crescent-shaped treats to celebrate after the city won a battle against the Ottoman Turks. The croissant shape came from the half-moon design on the Ottoman flag. When Austrians ate croissants, it was as if they were pretending to swallow their enemy!

Austrians love pastries. One of the best-known creations from Austria is the sachertorte, a chocolate cake covered with apricot jam and chocolate icing. This tasty treat was invented by a chef at the Sacher Hotel in Vienna.

Two other foods that are popular in Austria are wiener schnitzel, breaded veal cutlet; and backhendl, golden fried chicken.

Sachertorte

Wiener schnitzel

A Lipizzaner performing in Austria

Animals

One of the world's most skillful and beautiful horses comes from Austria. The **Lipizzaner** is an intelligent horse famous for its appearances at the Spanish Riding School in Vienna. Well-dressed riders take the horses around an arena to display their excellent skills.

Some great pets also come from Austria. The **Austrian short hair pinscher** is a very loyal and friendly dog. It weighs only about 30 pounds (13.6 kilograms), but is powerful for its size.

Bavarian mountain hound

The **Bavarian mountain hound** is a medium-sized hunting dog that many people keep as a house pet. It is a cross between the old Bavarian hound and the Tyrolean hound. It has a reddish and yellowish coat. It is very brave and obedient and is a loving pet.

Austrian short hair pinscher

23

A person dressed
up for Fasching

Child with treat
during Fasching

Child with treat
during Fasching

Holidays

Austrians love to celebrate a holiday called
Fasching. It's the Austrian version of Carnival,
a festival of parties, parades, and merrymaking
held every year in many European and Latin
American countries. Fasching begins on
New Year's Eve and usually lasts until February.

   In many ways, Fasching is like Halloween
because people dress up in interesting
costumes and pretend to be someone else.
Children get candies in the shapes of pigs,
gold coins, four-leaf clovers, and horseshoes.

People celebrating Fasching

The custom of celebrating Fasching comes from the Roman Catholic practice of feasting before beginning Lent. Lent is a 40-day period of fasting in preparation for Easter. Wearing costumes during Fasching gives people the freedom to act in ways that ordinarily would not be proper.

A recipe from Austria

Buchteln

Austrians like to eat different kinds of breads and rolls for breakfast, including treats called **Buchteln.** These are little rolls filled with jelly or jam. They're very easy to make, but require an adult to help bake them in the oven.

What you'll need:

- 16 pieces of frozen dinner-roll dough, thawed
- 1 cup of jelly or jam—choose your favorite flavor
- 4 tablespoons of butter, melted
- powdered sugar
- flour
- 10-inch cake pan
- rolling pin

1. Sprinkle a cutting board with flour. Place the pieces of dough on top and cover them with a towel. Place the dough in a warm spot to let it rise until it is double in size. You can also put the dough in an oven at 180 degrees to help it rise. Check the dough often so it does not cook.
2. When dough is ready, preheat the oven to 350 degrees.
3. Grease a 10-inch cake pan.
4. Sprinkle flour on a flat surface and roll each piece of dough into a square piece that is 4 inches by 4 inches.
5. Put a tablespoon of jelly or jam on the center of each square.
6. Put a little water on the edges of each square and pull up two of the corners. Pinch them closed with your fingers. Then pull up the other corners. Make sure all the seams are closed.
7. Place the squares in the baking pan. Brush the pieces with melted butter.

8. Cover the pan with the towel for about 20 minutes to let it rise a little more.

9. Take off the towel. Ask an adult to put the pan in the oven for about 30 minutes, or until the squares are lightly browned. When they are done, have an adult take them out of the oven. Let the pan cool for about five minutes, then have an adult take the squares out of the pan.

10. Place the squares on a wire rack and sprinkle them with powdered sugar.

11. Let the squares cool before pulling them apart. Enjoy!

27

How do you say....?

German and English come from the same family of languages.
As you can see, some German words are similar to English words.

English	German	How to pronounce it
good morning	guten Tag	GOOT-en TAAK
goodbye	auf Wiedersehen	owf-VEE-der-zay-en
thank you	danke	DAHNK-e
cake	Kuchen	KOOK-en
coffee	Kaffee	KAHF-ee
dog	Hund	huhnd
holiday	Feiertag	FIRE-tahg
horse	Pferd	faird
salt	Salz	zahltz
ski	Ski	ski
song	Lied	leed
waltz	Walzer	VAHL-zer

To find out more

Here are some other resources to help you learn more about Austria:

Books

Bergaami, Andrea and Cappor, Manuela. **Beethoven and the Classical Age** (Masters of Music). Barrons Juvenile, 1999.

Geography Department. **Austria in Pictures** (Visual Geography Series). Lerner Publications Co., 1992.

Sheehan, Sean. **Austria** (Cultures of the World). Benchmark Books, 1995.

Stein, R. Conrad. **Austria** (Enchantment of the World, Second Series). Children's Press, 2000.

Stein, R. Conrad. **Vienna** (Cities of the World). Children's Press, 1999.

Organizations and Online Sites

Austrian albums
http://www.aeiou.at/aeiou
A great site with an encyclopedia of Austria, collection of photos, music samples of famous classical works, a video, design and architecture information, and links to other sites.

CIA World Factbook: Austria
http://www.odci.gov/cia/ publications/factbook/geos/au.html
This site provides information on Austria's people, geography, government, economy, and more.

Lonely Planet Guide Destination Austria
http://www.lonelyplanet.com/dest/ eur/aus.htm
Lots of great information about visiting Austria, with some history, maps, cultural information, and recommended reading.

Microsoft Expedia, Austria
http://www.expedia.msn.com/wg/ Europe/Austria/P1295.asp
A helpful site for both travelers and people interested in Austria, with maps, history, geography, news, and vacation ideas.

Glossary

bellows a flexible device that pushes out air when squeezed

blood transfusion the transferring of blood from one person into the vein of another person

characteristic special quality or appearance that makes a person or thing different from others

chemical a substance formed when two or more substances act upon one another

choir a group of people who sing together, often in a church

choral sung by a choir

determine to be the cause of or reason for

diverse different, varied

emotional of or relating to the emotions

fasting choosing to not eat for a certain period of time

inherit to receive from one's parents or ancestors

offspring children

opera a musical play in which the actors sing all their lines

psychiatrist a doctor who helps people with emotional problems or diseases of the mind

technique a way of doing something

unconscious the part of the mind that does not usually enter a person's awareness and that is made known by such things as slips of the tongue or dreams

Index

accordion, 10

Auenbrugger, Leopold, 14

Austrian short hair pinscher, 22

backhendl, 20

Bavarian mountain hound, 23

Beethoven, Ludwig van, 7

blood typing, 16

Brahms, Johannes, 8

Buchteln, 26

chemical drugs, 14

chest-tapping technique, 14

classical composers, 6

classical music, 4, 6, 8

croissants, 20

"Edelweiss," 32

Fasching, 24

genetics, 15

German, 4

Haydn, Franz Joseph, 8

Landsteiner, Karl, 16

Lipizzaner, 22

Mahler, Gustav, 8

Mendel, Gregor, 15

metal ski bindings, 12

modern downhill skiing, 12

Mozart, Wolfgang Amadeus, 6

Paracelsus von Hohenheim, 14

psychoanalysis, 17

sachertorte, 20

salt mines, 18

Salzburg, 14, 18

Schneider, Hannes, 13

Schubert, Franz, 8

Sigmund Freud, 17

"Silent Night," 11

snow skiing, 12

Strauss, Johann Jr., 8

Strauss, Johann Sr., 8

Vienna, 6, 7, 10, 19, 20, 22, 29

Viennese coffee, 19

waltz, 8, 28

wiener schnitzel, 20

Zdarsky, Matthias, 12

Look what doesn't come from Austria!

Many people believe that the song **"Edelweiss"** is the national anthem of Austria. But it's really a song from a popular musical called *The Sound of Music,* about an Austrian family. Americans Oscar Hammerstein II and Richard Rodgers wrote "Edelweiss" in 1959. The real national anthem of Austria is called "Land der Berge, Land am Strome." It means "Land of Mountains, Land of Rivers."

Meet the Author

Kevin Davis loves to travel and write about the interesting places he has visited. He is a journalist and author who lives in Chicago. This book is dedicated to Miles, Rengin, Azize, and Julian.